CW01522299

EMPATH RISING

Remember why you came: the book to wake up your soul

Mandy Wheeler

BALBOA.PRESS

A DIVISION OF HAY HOUSE

Balboa Press books may be ordered through booksellers or by contacting:

Balboa Press
A Division of Hay House
1663 Liberty Drive
Bloomington, IN 47403
www.balboapress.co.uk
UK TFN: 0800 0148647 (Toll Free inside the UK)
UK Local: (02) 0369 56325 (+44 20 3695 6325 from outside the UK)

Print information available on the last page.

ISBN: 978-1-9822-8910-2 (sc)
ISBN: 978-1-9822-8909-6 (e)

Library of Congress Control Number: 2024918989

Balboa Press rev. date: 09/19/2024

CONTENTS

Mandy Wheeler is a spiritual teacher who has specialised in teaching other empaths how to understand their own abilities for over 15 years. Mandy is a psychic empath who offers spirit connection and future readings. She is a counsellor, regression therapist, clinical hypnotherapist and a healer.

She uses her training and abilities to assist other people in gaining their own personal power and connecting to their higher self.

This book is dedicated to my loving grandparents, Betty and Harold Cole, who ensured that books were a huge part of my childhood, and never had a day off from teaching me.

It is also dedicated to my paternal grandfather, John C. Hayes, an author himself with many published books. He has assisted me from the spirit world in writing this book.

Artwork by Kerry Darby

Mandy runs a virtual training group which teaches about energy and psychic development. She helps others to understand their own abilities and how to use it to the highest good of themselves and others.

To join the VIP group please visit her website: www.thespiritsway.co.uk and navigate to 'VIP Area'

CHAPTER ONE

ARE YOU AN EMPATH?

An empath is reactive to the energy of others and does not have the same filters a non-empath has, and this results in us absorbing energies of others (whether they are positive or negative) into our own energy field, this creates an experience for us that if we become fully aware and functioning allows for us to understand others at a very deep level.

I was the age of 34 when I discovered I was an empath and although prior to this I had absolutely no knowledge that us empaths existed I was very aware that I was highly sensitive and tuned in to others very deeply.

Looking back at my childhood and younger years I realised this ability had been with me from when I can first remember and there is absolutely no doubt in my mind that it caused me to create many life changing events as a young adult which impacted my future enormously, I am quite confident that if I had understood these abilities and became aware at an earlier point in my life there would have been many situations which would have turned out quite differently however my guides and spirit helpers decided that I was on a journey of discovery and without all of the steps along the way my story would not be quite the same and neither would yours so it's important to remember that we always come to points in our life exactly when we are supposed to.

In those early days of acceptance it would consistently replay on my mind that I could not possibly have these abilities despite the fact that my daily life was proving otherwise, I spent the next 9 years studying with my guides and took the time to learn as much as I possibly could about myself and my new found skills, I chose to dedicate these years to study of self and with the exception of work and caring for my children I spent as much time alone as possible in order to delve into my own shadow work. This in turn led me to train myself in reading energy which remains my passion in life.

Learning to understand that you can feel people's pain and emotion is absolutely mind-blowing and quite unbelievable. I had been reading cards and working clairvoyantly for around 5 years already, however I did not know how it all worked really, I did not have a knowledge of understanding how I was able to read the future at that point. My journey into training and understanding myself as an empath taught me that peoples energy and thoughts talk to me and as the years passed my knowledge continued to grow which has allowed me to truly understand just how connected we all are.

Being an empath allows for a clear advantage to navigate your relationships with others as long as you are an aware and functioning one. Any empath who remains unaware will find life to be extremely difficult, due to the fact that although they have been born with the same set of skills as an empath who has become aware their level of comprehension will not be the same, therefore creating blocks and difficulties at every turn.

All of us begin life as unaware empaths unless we are lucky enough to be born into a spiritual family who themselves are aware of what it means and how to work with it to the highest good. An empath child will be a painful soul due to the fact that they will be consistently absorb their environment, they will not be equipped with the knowledge that this is in any way different to other people, so they will create themselves based upon the version of whose energy they are absorbing along with who is responsible for their conditioning. For this reason others will notice the drastic behaviour changes with them more than with non-empaths, especially as they head into their teenage years and start gaining more freedom and stronger relationships in new groups.

When an empath is unaware, they will display signs of fatigue and feeling drained. Others may also find that they seem to have a real sadness about them, they will be equipped with a real sense of knowing what people around their lives need and will show a very caring and sensitive side as a child. Their personality can either be changeable or seem to be almost a carbon copy of their primary caregivers, and whilst many will presume this is genetics, a large proportion of it is contributed to their empath ability.

As we go through life our higher self will offer us more than one opportunity to understand our abilities, however, not all of us will take notice of this and sadly this leaves some empaths living a life of pain and torment with little knowledge of who they truly are.

The basic empath signs are as follows:

- **an innate ability to understand how somebody is feeling without being told**
- **the ability to read the energy of a room**
- **understanding somebody's emotions and feelings towards yourself or others**
- **outbursts of energy for no reason**
- **feeling sad or angry completely out of the blue**
- **being impacted by an interaction with someone else for no reason**
- **being completely drained by others**

signs that you are a more advanced empath will include

- **feeling the medical ailments of others**
- **hearing the thoughts of others**
- **reading an empty room through layers of energy**
- **channelling energy of people who are not in your presence**
- **channelling and reading energy of those you think of without connecting to them**
- **having a clear and cognizant knowledge of who somebody is in their soul.**

If you feel that you identify with all of these signs then you are an empath and will benefit greatly from reading this book, if you feel you are an unaware empath then gaining knowledge alongside a tool kit will allow for you to make life changing adaptions to how you currently deal with a sensory overload along with a clear knowledge of how to disconnect from others in order to be fully present in your own energy.

Empathic illnesses can be extremely hard to cope with as although you do not actually have this illness your body or mind will be telling you otherwise, many empaths are labelled as hypochondriac's.

There is an ability in this when you begin to realise it, if you flip it from *'everybody is physically destroying me and there is nothing I can do about it'* around to *'I have the ability to help people to understand that they have a physical illness in their body and where the root cause is'* then you begin to understand why you came here to earth with these abilities.

Every single problem which an empath endures is actually a positive ability with a purpose. When you have begun your journey to understand yourself and that in which you can assist humanity with it, it stops becoming painful and you will cease to feel the need for survival from this amazing ability which you carry.

As you progress through the book it will become evident to you that my teachings are primarily focused on healing of self, and this will equip you with the knowledge you will need for you to understand where your blockages lie. Without these blockages in the way your ability to become a clear medical intuitive is strong (and you will save yourself a lot of trips to the doctors) with your new level of awareness.

Learning to read the health of others will over time become second nature if you are a physical empath. It is important when you do so to ensure that you are cleansing your own energy, otherwise you will absorb these issues with your spongelike energy field creating an imbalance within your own vibration.

Mental health can be a difficult empath illness to channel as it affects our mind as well as physically, therefore creating more questions. For the unaware empath this can become a very scary time.

It is important to keep yourself separate from the person who you are channelling, whether that is intentional or unintentional, as keeping a clear divide in your mind about who you are and who they are will help you to detach yourself from this energy.

I have wrote a chapter on etheric cords later in the book which offers healthy ways of detaching from energy.

Shielding or psychic protection will allow for you to maintain a level of control regarding absorbing the energy of others.

In order to shield you will need to practice over time as we are all different and some of us are more visual than others. Try to imagine that you are being placed within a large egg or bubble of light, you can choose the colour but be aware some colours are more protective than others, in my experience gold light and purple light tend to be highly protective.

Try to visualise your shield so that you are totally encased in it, it should be a few inches from your body in order to protect your auric field.

Over time you may find that you get quite adept at knowing intuitively when you must put up your shield, this will help you to build up your own strength in your vibrational field.

Empaths are here on earth to assist humanity, however

due to the nature of how we offer that help, a large amount of us are manipulated, hurt and trodden down. This is ultimately our own doing due to the fact that we are either unaware or we refuse to change our mindset and truly come into your power.

By coming into our power, it is not my intention to teach you only how to survive as an empath, it is my intention that I assist you to learn to soar and to remember why you came to earth and what your purpose is.

We did not plan a life of martyrdom, wasting our abilities. We came here to assist each other on our own individual journeys, and I am clear that it is my purpose in life - to help as many people as I can to fulfil their purpose.

The beginning of our empath journey can be daunting and confusing, however when we truly begin to realise how deep the connection is between all of us humans on earth and begin to understand the collective consciousness at a deeper level, there comes a clarity which takes away all of our questioning and our inability to understand how we form these connections.

The realisation that we are all part of the same source energy allows for us to explore our abilities with a knowledge that we are protected.

Mandy Wheeler

_____

_____

_____

_____

_____

_____

_____

_____

_____

_____

_____

_____

_____

_____

_____

_____

_____

_____

_____

_____

_____

_____

_____

_____

_____

_____

_____

_____

_____

_____

_____

Mandy Wheeler

Mandy Wheeler

_____
_____
_____
_____
_____
_____
_____
_____
_____
_____
_____
_____
_____
_____
_____
_____
_____
_____
_____
_____
_____
_____
_____
_____
_____
_____
_____

Chapter Two

MY OWN EXPERIENCES

Waking up changed my entire human experience by assisting me not only on my spiritual journey but also on my human journey.

I feel it's important to share my experiences as they have led me to gain the knowledge which I hold today, and it is my personal belief that the journey is always more important than the destination.

My childhood was not what you would call the norm. Today, nobody would have blinked an eye, but back then we were viewed as very different. I grew up with my grandparents from around the age of 18 months old, and I was always aware that the circumstances leading to this situation left my parents with very little alternative. Whilst my parents were still in my life, it did very little to alleviate the trauma which would later come back to haunt me from this situation.

I hear lots of empath discussions where people state that being an empath is a direct result of Childhood trauma. Whilst I would agree that most empaths whom I cross paths with in my work have experienced trauma, I am hesitant to believe that an empath is a product of their environment.

Empaths come to earth with the most amazing and selfless abilities which undoubtedly causes us untold damage, however for us to determine that these abilities are a direct result of trauma is taking away our power and labelling our ability as a disability.

I do not personally get on board with this theory for a number of reasons: one of those reasons being that we are here to spread love and to mirror the experiences of our fellow humans, so surely it stands to reason that if we were a product of our trauma, this would not be the case.

What all of these theorists seem to have either forgotten, or were never aware of in the first place, is that we have come to earth with a divine plan which we decided as a soul. Whilst we were in our in between lives states we shared goals and growth strategies with our soul group with a plan to lead us to the lessons which we must experience in this lifetime now.

What the theorists are actually in fact doing is separating the human experience from the soul, which in my opinion and experience, does not make any sense on a spiritual level.

My memories of spiritual connections alongside channelling energy were happening as early as I can remember. As a young child, I was experiencing astral travel, which I now feel incorporated some of my past lives. These can be interpreted by people who are less spiritually minded as imagination.

It is my belief that there is room for a lot of research into this area if we wish to start understanding the absolute truth about time and dimensions.

The sadness and upset which I would channel as a child were extremely destructive. I was not yet aware of any spiritual abilities, and no matter how wonderful my grandparents were, like most families they came with their own issues and their own baggage. They had both been active in World War 2 which undoubtedly left them with, what we now know as, PTSD.

My grandmother was quite a tough lady. For me, an empath who was already building up rejection issues, this was always going to make for a difficult mix. My sister and I would both give different accounts of our childhood. Not factually of course, but emotionally, as we both would be taking different lessons from our experience, and this is due to the differences in our emotions and in how we perceive the world.

I recollect how sad I would become regularly in my childhood home and looking back I am aware that some of this sadness was my own feelings created by rejection. However, some of the sadness was also the absorbing of energy.

The reasons that my rejection issues were constantly being reaffirmed, was due to a number of reasons. One of these reasons being that my mom was still on the scene and she would visit us. These visits did not feel to be structured or regular, however, I *was* a young child so I may have had an unreal perception of time.

I remember clearly how I would spend days at the window waiting and could not understand my grandparents anger. I now know that they were angry because they felt we were experiencing hurt and rejection on a regular basis. This was not intentional on my mom's part, but she led a very unstructured and busy life which obviously impacted us.

At around the age of 7 years old, my mom arrived one day to visit - with a baby. We were informed that we had a little sister. This was so confusing for us and led to deeper rejection issues which over time buried deep as we could not comprehend why our sister was allowed to live with our mom but we was not.

My parents had separated many years earlier and my dad would visit regularly, bringing us contact with the paternal side of the family also.

I remember clearly throughout my childhood that every time my mom visited, I would sit on her lap and apologise. It became a bit of a running joke if I remember correctly, and no one seemed to understand what I was sorry for. It is quite clear to me now that I felt the need to apologise for not being good enough.

This cycle continued and unbeknown to the child version of me this was setting the scene for some extremely deep-rooted rejection issues which would help to form the adult I would become.

As I lived with my grandparents in a time that everybody else had parents, we were singled out as different and this also reflected materially. My grandparents were on a pension, so money was something which they had to be very careful with. They were bringing up 2 children at a time in their lives when they were only financially equipped to care for themselves.

I was bullied as a child in primary school. I was made to feel different and not good enough. I felt isolated, ugly and embarrassed of who I was. This led me to be so withdrawn and self-conscious, that I did not understand who I was. It would be a long time before I did. I was painfully aware that I was the last person picked for team work, and I could feel the pity from the teachers as I absorbed it .

I was different and that had to be a bad thing, right?

I would not understand for many years that I was absorbing all of this energy and sadness too. Apart from what was being created on a mental and emotional level, there were also patterns forming. Patterns of not only my own stuff, but also the absorbing of the energy around me, which was creating another different version of myself almost layered on top of the negative emotional conditioning.

I was an anxious and fearful child, and I cannot remember a point that I did not experience these emotions. I now understand that I had an anxiety disorder.

My nan liked a drink twice a week and it was on these days that I found life difficult to cope with. I remember the crippling emotions and sadness that used to flow through me and lead me to spend the evenings crying on my bed. Although there may have been the odd time that I was shouted at or told off, most times I just could not cope with how I was feeling. I just internalised it all and over time that sadness became my sadness.

I still remember the day that our world was blown apart like it was yesterday. The police had been sent to our school due to a malicious letter they had received.

We arrived home to see our nan crying and scared, she did not know what to do and just like anybody in those days she took the option of what she felt was safety.

My uncle had been diagnosed with schizophrenia and not too long before this instance, he had given my grandparents reason to ban him from our house. He had attempted to be inappropriate to us. He took great offence at this. He made up false lies about my grandad, who I can say to this day was the most amazing man I have ever known.

This situation struck fear into my nan. She thought that we would be taken from her, so we were sent to live with my mom that very night.

This incident changed my grandad overnight, and it broke his heart. We were not aware, obviously, at that point of how much damage his own son had caused him, but we still believe to this day that he triggered the massive brain haemorrhage that he was to have only 18 months later.

We were now in a very bittersweet situation as we finally had what every child wants. We had our mom. But our nan had become our mom, so in the blink of an eye, as it was that fast, we were leaving the secure and loving home of one mom into the alien environment of another mom. An environment that was so completely different to our only known childhood home. We were also gaining another sister to live with, who we had not really had the opportunity to build any type of relationship with. It was all to come with a whole heap of fireworks and lifechanging situations.

When I look back that was the very day that I said goodbye to the scared and anxious version of me - the version who wore the rejection I felt on my sleeve.

Our new life was one of spontaneity and constant rushing around. We had none of the structure which we had become accustomed to, and for an empath this is like a full on assault on the sensory system.

Within the first few weeks, my whole personality changed and I became more defiant against life in general.

It is only now, as I write this book, that I realise I was absorbing and reacting to my mom's energy - as this is exactly who she is.

My first day of school was daunting - we had left a small junior school but, in the area, we now lived they went to senior school a lot earlier. We now headed to a huge 3 storey double building senior school, this was absolutely terrifying for us and I can honestly say this day is etched on my memory. I got through the day quite unscathed from being in such a huge environment with a completely different system to how we knew schooling to be, I later became aware that I was in some type of autopilot mode at this stage in my life, unable to process anything .

We headed into the door, excited to tell our mom about all the new things which we had learned. We walked into a room filled with bikers. My moms partner was a biker, and there were 4 of his friends there when we returned home. They were all drinking.

We lived in a terraced house so there were 2 reception rooms. As we ran through to the second reception room to greet her, we were met by her with blood dripping down her face and big bruising where he had hit her. Naturally, we began to cry and get upset as we had never witnessed this before and was completely unaware of what was going on. This was to be the first time of many.

It was never open for discussion so we were forced to just accept it and adapt, leaving us now in a domestic violence household 2 weeks in to losing our home and security.

I was now a very different person to the girl who had moved in a short while ago and my personality changed almost instantly. I can definitely see how I absorbed my environment leading to me becoming a totally different person than I was prior to this. I was now being conditioned again, but this time, it was in a totally different way. I was to channel my rejection in a completely different way too, using it as wall and barrier to keep me safe.

It was not until my 3rd child at the age of 30 was born that I began working on my defence mechanisms and realising what they were and why. I understand that throughout my teenage years and my twenties, I was still carrying a lot of my mom's energy. This definitely brought me some positivity in my coping mechanisms, but also taught me to hide a lot from myself.

In those early years, life had changed drastically, which was going to pretty much determine my future and also the future of my own children. As the book progresses, you will understand how the child empath becoming the adult empath faces numerous internal battles in a quest for any type of peace within.

Within the schooling environment, I became loud and rebellious, and it seemed nothing mattered to me now. It was only a matter of time before I felt the need to escape in other ways. Before the age of 12, I was smoking regularly, and I had begun escaping my new found life experiences through substance abuse. I felt the need to escape - my sensory overload by now was at a catastrophic stage, I had no idea who I was anymore and had become defiant and argumentative, purely for the sake of it. Again, I am now aware this was a pattern created by myself based upon a false version of the energy I was channelling and keeping for myself.

My mom was and still is a fighter. This obviously means

I will inherit genes, as we all do, however at the age of 13 and with the previous personality of meekness and being a yes person only months earlier, it shows how environment can cause such massive changes in an empath's personality.

By the age of 13, my school career was completely over. By the time I started my first job at the age of 15, the substance abuse was in my past. I consider myself extremely lucky, and I feel this is down to my guides strong connection with myself.

It was around this time that my wonderful grandad who I had been very close to and felt understood by, died of a brain haemorrhage. *This was when I was to see my first spirit.*

My grandad was standing at the bottom of my bed and the most amazing white lights were shining from him – the most amazing that I've ever seen to this day. At this point in my life I was a teenager who was into all the wrong things and was very negative, so it would be a long time in the future before I would really accept and understand this spiritual interaction. It was during these years after my grandad's passing that I noticed a pattern emerging where I just seemed to know things. Then these things began actually happening and I had no understanding or knowledge about anything psychic or spiritual. My grandparents had not been spiritual in any way, or if they had, they had never openly discussed it with us.

My dad was and still is very spiritual but as I grew up with my grandparents it was not something which he had ever had the opportunity to teach me about at this stage. I didn't delve into this any further and life carried on in quite a normal way from this point onwards, where at the age of 16 I left home and moved into my own flat.

These years didn't really show me any psychic phenomenon's or any spiritual encounters, however looking back, I am aware that I was absorbing energy and making life choices and decisions very rashly based upon my inability to understand that I was able to channel others. When I look back now, I see so many situations where I was actually being completely led by others energy.

At the age of 19 I became pregnant with my first child. It's here at this point that some of my earlier trauma and upsets began to manifest. My protection towards my daughter was fierce and I was terrified that I would lose her. I could not believe that I would be allowed to keep somebody in my life who I had that level of love for, and this manifested in a real anxiety which I was not aware of at that point.

I was so scared that I would lose her, I slept on the floor in the lounge for weeks of her life as I was terrified of cot death. Now I can see how silly that was, but in my brain, if I did not go to bed it could not happen. I swore to my daughter from the moment of conception that no one would ever scare her or make her fearful, and this began a pattern with me throughout all of my children's upbringings.

Her father was quite verbally aggressive and there was a lot of shouting. I had sworn that none of my children would ever experience what I did so I left. My daughter spent time in her teenage years acknowledging that if I had stayed with him, her life would have been more negative and thanked me for making the decision I did. Now don't get me wrong, he was a wonderful dad, and she loves him very much, however it would not have made for a happy home.

I am grateful for my childhood experiences as it ensured

that I would understand life as a child in a toxic environment. It is this understanding which has ensured that I have made decisions with my children's emotional wellbeing at the forefront over the years, regarding the environment they were raised in.

The birth of my 2nd child caused major empathic anxiety disorder.

In the 5th month of pregnancy my clairvoyant abilities seemed to reappear creating some very confusing situations for me. I would constantly be told psychically that I was to have a post-partum haemorrhage which I had never heard of.

I was not aware at this point that I was psychic, so I felt quite concerned about my own mental health, but when I gave birth to him, I did in fact have a post-partum haemorrhage, which took me a very long time to recover from.

At this point in my life, I brought a house and at the same time my niece was sadly born with a chromosome disorder, who at the age of 6 months old, died. This stage in my life was difficult, to say the least, however it was being made more difficult by the unknown fact that the pregnancy of my son had somehow triggered my empath ability tenfold.

After studying and gaining understanding of this I became aware that it is due to him also being an empath which was mirroring myself, therefore enhancing my own ability.

I was later to understand that some illnesses which I was experiencing at this point in my life was the channelling of the lady who, unbeknown to me, had died in the house before I brought it. Instead of opening up to my abilities at this point, I became overwhelmed by them causing me a very difficult time empathically which the medical field could not comprehend.

The pregnancy of my 3rd son kickstarted my interest in healing and spirituality. I had already began reading tarot cards at this point but my spiritual knowledge was limited. My youngest son is also an empath with a clairvoyant ability.

As an empath who is autistic and very deep, his struggle is big. He seems to be coping well and although the learning curves have been huge, he is very knowledgeable of self, with a very intense level of spirituality. I have absolutely no doubt that if he had not been born to me I would not have gained as much knowledge as I have in these fields. Some souls are old wise souls, and he is most definitely a teacher to me and has brought me a lot of the knowledge which I have been lucky enough to learn over these years.

It is important for us to remember that each soul who we interact with and become connected to will bring us lessons and only when we look for these lessons will we learn as we had planned to before we came.

Over the years, I found that letting people in and letting people love or care for me was extremely difficult. I developed patterns in relationships which would see me push away anybody who wanted to get really close. It wasn't until I started training as a counsellor that the lid was lifted on this can of worms and luckily for me this resulted in me gaining knowledge of a major rejection issue which stemmed from early life maternal separation and abandonment. I seem to have hidden this extremely well from myself over the years as I became the rejector due to not understanding my real true reasons for running. I learned through my healing work that I was running before I could be hurt or rejected again, and the reason for this was I felt that nobody could love me. I felt that once they really knew who I was, they would leave me, because in my subconscious if my mom didn't want to stay then surely no one else would.

As an adult I have been very aware for my entire life that my mom loved me and wanted me, however the subconscious of a child cannot comprehend fact.

The second major trauma trigger manifested with each of my children's fathers which I have already briefly mentioned, my children all have different fathers due to this very fact and I found that running away was easier than trying to work together to understand the feelings I was going through.

As a young mother I had made a conscious decision that nobody would ever make my children feel scared or uncomfortable in their own home because my belief that the home must be a place where they can truly relax and feel safe and needs to be a sanctuary had been reinforced in my younger years.

This was a definite internal defence system which had been created from both aspects of my childhood, my grandmother drank regularly and the effects of being around drink led to a dislike of alcohol and as my mom's abusive partner was also a heavy drinker. This then created a reality for me that drink led to violence and fear

Until I was in my mid-30s, I would drink when socialising, however I had always been extremely uncomfortable when any of my partners drank alcohol, which led to some very difficult emotions for me to deal with. Two of the relationships which I ran from was a direct result of my children being affected through either anger or control and I found this very easy to do.It is only now through the shadow work which I have done on my triggers that I no longer run as I have healed from the experiences which saw me live life in survival mode .

I have shared some of my experiences purely because this book is an authentic representation of all which I have learned over the years and without these traumas there would be no reason for my healing.

My understanding of the shadow work which I have needed to do has led me to be able to help others in their journey with their own healing and I am eternally grateful that my experiences along with my guides help make this possible.

An empath will always become their environment and when you understand this your journey becomes visible.

_____

_____

_____

_____

_____

_____

_____

_____

_____

_____

_____

_____

_____

_____

_____

_____

_____

_____

_____

_____

_____

_____

_____

_____

_____

_____

_____

_____

_____

_____

_____

CHAPTER THREE

UNLEARNING OUR HUMAN PROGRAMME.

As we progress on our souls journey to enlightenment the continuous raising of our vibration equips us with an innate desire to completely eradicate all of the human teachings which we have been indoctrinated into however in order for us to remove our conditioning it is necessary for us to first unlearn the human programming and in doing so it will assist us to elevate and begin our soul journey.

I feel patterns is an important step as by allowing ourselves to become aware of the patterns which we have created throughout our life and relationship's we begin to unravel a thread which has led us into a deep sleep.

As you are reading this book you will already be aware that we as humans have been asleep and now as we head into the golden age more and more of us are waking up, however in order for us to become fully awake to our abilities and our true purpose we must reconnect with our soul which will allow for our higher self to lead us and by doing so we begin the amazing and life changing process of un learning the human programming.

The beginning of this process will help us to recognize the patterns which we have formed and I will go into detail regarding patterns a bit later on but at this stage I would just like to briefly cover how our own self tends to form and nurture a pattern which we create.

From the moment we enter this world we are being conditioned by other human beings who are mainly our caregivers and society itself, of course this is not possible to avoid in any way as we are incapable of taking care of ourselves at this point or making our own decisions.

We are taught how to walk, talk and behave and what this actually does is it takes away the Freedom of our soul which is innocent in human ways and leaves us to rely completely upon those people around us to shape us and guide us on this human journey.

Whilst many of the teaching's which we receive may bring positive and light to our life for some it will give their soul one of the biggest battles that they could ever face.

As we grow we are forming into the version of ourselves which our parents or caregivers, teachers, siblings and peers believe we should be and without realising this we are a creation of all of these peoples beliefs and rules, in turn as we become adults we form relationships and create partnerships which then have the capacity to mould us to become a different version of this again.

For those people who are unlucky enough to cross paths with or become emotionally involved with a narcissistic personality type we could end up in a potentially soul damaging cycle for many lifetimes.

There will be intermittent times that some of us rebel as our soul will be trying to become free however many people at this point are labelled as troublemakers and the journey can be tough, these people are the way showers and should be celebrated however sadly in our Society they struggle in the early years often suppressing their inner wisdom as society just wants them to be quiet and conform.

The key here is to embrace the rebellion which you feel and learn to honour it, the fact that you're reading this book already tells me that your awareness of feelings and empathy is high and by allowing yourself to follow your own inner guidance and tune in deeply to your senses navigating your own sensory system will become easy therefore enabling you to identify what feels right and what feels wrong for your soul.

We are born and placed into a system which has been designed for us to follow it with no questions asked but by asking questions we break down the blind acceptance of being told who we should be and the conditioning which is placed upon us.

As we have now made the conscious decision that we are on our path to remembering who we are we need to focus on how to unlearn all which we have been told we are and i find a good starting point is to identify your own belief system.

This exercise will alert you to whether or not this belief system belongs to you or if it is a replica of your primary caregivers or partners own beliefs? I would suggest that you make a list, this list should be comprised of all which we feel controls us and holds us back from fully embracing our soul.

The list should begin as far back as the memory allows you should first focus on remembering all of the things which have made you feel sad,this is a relatively easy place to begin, after you have covered this list everything which has caused fear, worry, financial restrictions and health concerns for example and then move on to the bigger issues at hand such as rejection, abandonment and any type of abuse as these are the real root issues which are mainly at the core of most of the other blocks in our life.

It is important to visit all the emotions which you will be experiencing at this point with the emphasis on the emotions which may make you feel guilty for questioning everything which others felt was right to teach you.

Do not be afraid to feel confused or to question things which may elicit a feeling of anger or upset, these are important emotions to explore during this exercise and I find that meditating upon this will help you to understand how the conditioning still impacts you.

By understanding the actions and emotions that this triggers it will place you in a much stronger position to enable change and healing if you feel that healing is something which you choose to incorporate.

In order to implement change, it is vital to be true to yourself and not to allow any feelings of guilt towards anybody for honouring your feelings.

It is important to take action in your daily life in regard to unlearning conditioning, Becoming observant of your own actions and emotional responses will ensure that you can be aware when you are repeating the pattern of continuation.

Remind yourself that you are no longer that person and that you wish to replace the specific emotion or action with your own desired alternative, within 3 to 4 weeks you should begin to have an awareness of the new reality which you are creating being conditioned into your daily routine.

When we open our eyes to the causes of all which keeps us rooted to the indoctrination we can then begin to remove the barriers to accessing our soul at a deep level and please understand this will be a painful process which could cause some breakdowns in relationships however this is going to be necessary as we should never allow for our links to other humans to hold us down on our journey of growth.

By becoming aware and unlearning all the patterns which make up the human version of us this will enable us to begin uncovering our real true soul which has been hidden or only partly visited.

It is now time to peel back the layers and identify with everything which lies beneath. This process will undoubtedly become an endless learning journey which if you're doing it right will continue throughout your entire lifetime here on Earth.

We are infinite beings who are multi-layered and when we begin to truly understand this, we can become deeply aware at a soul level that earth and all of its lessons are merely a stepping stone.

What all of this unlearning will eventually bring is the peeling back of layers and in this process you will begin to remove heavier energy which will then create a higher vibration resulting in the removal of the lower vibrational energy which you have been accumulating and creating throughout your lifetime on earth as this energy will no longer be a vibrational match.

As your vibration Raises your true empath ability will become stronger and whilst this means you will feel even more deeply it will also teach you how to gain more control over it which will in turn enable you to become more aware and adept at managing to keep the energy of others on the outside of your energy field.

As you begin to grow as an empath this will assist you in uncovering skills which you are not yet aware of, being an aware empath holds many more skills than most empaths will understand until they truly begin to study themselves and it is at this point that the true reality of the connection we all have to each other gets revealed allowing for us to connect to each other and every person who we come into contact with on a whole different level.

I will be covering the exact level of the depth which we connect with each other later in the book but at this stage it is important to allow for yourself to understand that pretty much anything is possible, and this is imperative on your learning journey. Becoming an aware empath will enhance your life and allow for you to be fully in control of your own ability just as you intended when you signed up to come to earth.

_____
_____
_____
_____
_____
_____
_____
_____
_____
_____
_____
_____
_____
_____
_____
_____
_____
_____
_____
_____
_____
_____
_____
_____
_____
_____
_____
_____
_____
_____
_____
_____
_____
_____

_____
_____
_____
_____
_____
_____
_____
_____
_____
_____
_____
_____
_____
_____
_____
_____
_____
_____
_____
_____
_____
_____
_____
_____
_____
_____
_____

CHAPTER FOUR

WHOSE ENERGY IS THIS?

The biggest and most important question for an aware empath will always be: *'who's energy is this?'* and the reason for this is because we are constantly absorbing energy which we find ourselves carrying. This is not obvious to us all of the time which leaves us quite vulnerable to manipulation.

This manipulation is not always intentional however those people whom the empath trusts enough to share their abilities with are now placed in a position of power over the empath as if they wished to, they could lead the empath with their own energy.

There are many times that this is not intentional and the non-empath will see coincidence everywhere whilst not understanding how the empath truly works, the more aware an empath becomes the more it will allow for them to recognise these patterns within themselves and most times this will be enough for them to accept that they are channelling the energy of somebody else.

I am sure you can understand that this is the main reason why an empath's training is imperative as without this knowledge they will always be led by others thoughts and actions which on many occasions can have catastrophic results.

We can learn to read the energy of others quite easily once we have learned to understand our own energy and by doing so it helps to allow for us to create energetic boundaries.

Firstly, it is important to assess how aware you are of your own energy and whether you can recognise it. This will help for you to understand when you are acting out of character. This level of understanding will provide a trigger if you remain quite conscious of your ability to feel the emotions of others, this trigger is usually enough to remind you that you need to pull your energy back.

Over the years in my teachings, I have witnessed a lot of empath situations. Myself, along with some of my students, have become quite aware of how easily an Empath's energy field can expand and move from one person to another. It is important for us to gain knowledge of people's energy in order to serve us on our learning journey of becoming an awakened empath.

I learned from these experiences how an empath's energy enters the energy field of another person and this knowledge has assisted me greatly in being able to understand how I can help myself and other empaths to remain at our own vibrational level whilst helping others if it is our purpose here on earth to do so.

For many years I believed that people were placing their energy upon me, but in actual fact I was choosing to understand their experience at a deeper level as does all empaths. I feel that this knowledge has helped to build a protection structure, because by us being aware that we are making the choices this removes the myth of us being victims therefore allowing for us to understand the true level of faith and belief which we truly hold in our own power.

Power is key for any empath. This is generally something which we give away and convince ourselves that a situation which causes us energy blockages or draining is happening to us without our permission.

I have found with myself and many students that by keeping a journal of energy it helps for the person to develop a greater sense of understanding much quicker than those who don't keep one, this journal should contain all energy changes as well as who you have spent time with and how they were in themselves. By doing this for 1 month and then looking back at it, it will become apparent that there is a pattern of energy around certain people and this will assist you to understand the changes which will occur for you whenever you are in the company of each specific person.

We hold complete power over not only our human experience but also every choice and action which we take within this experience, by choosing to regain our own personal power our energy is then focused purely on where we choose to send it. When we spend our time constantly worrying and stressing how other people are impacting us so deeply and causing us to become drained then where do you think the energy is going to gravitate towards?

Of course, it will create more of the same as energy flows to energy therefore whatever you focus on you will only serve to create.

The empath holds an ability to manifest with ease and precision and this ability is only hampered by our own mind, when our mind is clear and full of clarity then we are an open channel which will allow for a free flow of energy throughout our energy system and chakra system.

So surely it is the obvious choice to understand that our energy will flow to whatever thought process we follow as everything, and everyone is made up of the same infinite energy.

The moment we stop seeing ourselves as the victims is the moment that we have chosen to take back our power and I can promise you with a bit of self-knowledge and training that you can be on a fast track to creating the version of you which you fully intended to be when you made the choice to come to earth.

The second most important thing you need to do as an empath is to raise your vibration, all of us here on earth are here for this very purpose and whilst it is paramount for all of us it is slightly more difficult for an empath, the reason for this is simply because we are picking up the energy of others continuously and in doing so it is not possible for us to abstain from creating new patterns which inherently belong to others.

The more energy which we accumulate and spend time in will in turn become our own energy over time and this is because if it is not cleared from our own energy field it will then cause us to have brought in a change to our own vibrational field.

The reason for this is because our vibration is a reflection of our own thoughts, actions, beliefs and patterns so therefore if we are accumulating the energy of others and not clearing it from our energy field it is quite obvious that there will be some lower level vibrations coming in at some point which in turn will drop our own vibration.

For us to lift our own vibration we must rid ourselves of all excess lower vibrational energy which will be stored not only in our own auric field but also in our chakra system. Fear, anxiety and stress build upon each other and the results of this will be that we are carrying around every negative situation and thought process which has ever been part of our story and whilst carrying this heavy baggage it is completely impossible for us to understand or know ourselves at a deep soul level.

Honesty is key here in order for you to raise your vibration as you cannot lie to yourself, and energy does not lie.

If you are still allowing lower vibrational frequencies to live within your vibrational field then it cannot raise. The way our vibration raises is to let go of all of the heavier thoughtforms and emotions. If you are carrying around guilt, hatred, envy and fear then you are going to have a lower vibration than those who are not as these are heavy energies with a dense frequency.

You must begin to start processing your own energy and understanding it, this in turn will allow for you to revisit the root of this particular energy and where it began, the only way to remove this energy is to heal it which requires that you face it and begin the process of acknowledging the effects it has upon you as a person.

By following this procedure with any lower vibrational emotions and thoughtforms which you have formed over your life you will be facilitating your own healing and therefore raising your own vibration.

When we begin to unpack and revisit our own issues we

are clearing the way and creating a space for our human to reconnect with our soul whilst allowing our body to become a clear vessel for our own channelling, once we have created a clear vessel within ourselves this will allow for us to truly know who we are and in turn this will allow for us to know when we are not ourselves.

This entire process gives us the insights and tools to understand the other person at a soul level with a very deep clarity of knowledge and only when we can understand somebody at this level can we be part of the process of assisting them in facilitating their own healing.

The raising of your vibration will be a continuous journey bringing you many lessons along the way and I find it is important to remember that we are all on the same journey.

It can get very frustrating when we have raised our own vibration and we feel that the vibration and behaviour of others is impacting us negatively but let's just remember that we are all of the same infinite energy and we are all here to assist each other to become the best version of who we can be whilst raising the vibration of earth.

Remember that you are a person who is capable of deep empathy, and I have complete faith that not only will you work for your own highest good but you will also help to lift others.

Mandy Wheeler

Mandy Wheeler

_____
_____
_____
_____
_____
_____
_____
_____
_____
_____
_____
_____
_____
_____
_____
_____
_____
_____
_____
_____
_____
_____
_____
_____
_____
_____
_____

CHAPTER FIVE

RECOGNISING PATTERNS

One of the most important observations for an empath is to recognise the patterns which we ourselves, along with other key people in our experience, have created. This is an integral part of our journey - by realising the patterns which have formed within our life we can start to understand which patterns are our own and which ones we seem to have inherited from others.

When we trace our behaviour, moral code, belief system and general perception of ourselves and the world back to its source then it will always begin with our caregivers from birth.

When we were born and throughout our primary years we did not have any control at all over the patterns which we began creating as we were taught to think, act, believe and behave in exactly the way our care giver's believed to be right. It is these patterns which have helped to form the people who we are today and who we believe ourselves to be. As we were growing our caregivers were the people who instilled in us what was right and wrong and taught us what to think and as children we gained a belief system which grew with us incorporating all of these patterns and beliefs which we continue to keep in our life today.

*I would like you to ask yourself if there was ever a point that you sat down and questioned whether the person who you are today is a result of conditioning and if the answer is no, **why?***

The reason I ask why is because an empath's knowledge and understanding of self is key to our ability to navigate earth as a functioning empath. When an empath does not understand who they are and why they are following a specific way of life then they will have no way of differentiating their own energy from the energy of others.

So how do patterns form?

It is quite a simple process really and whilst many people can grasp the concept of the mind creating patterns they don't give enough thought to the impact upon our energy system, when we repeat an action or a thought on a regular basis it is clear to see how this becomes a habit.

A habit is a pattern of behaviour or a pattern of thought and by us taking on these patterns from other people we are not being true to ourselves as we have formed a pattern within our life which may in fact be the opposite of who we truly are and what we came here to do.

What we rarely do as humans is to give time to truly understand how that repeated pattern arrived in the first place but if we did give time, we may very well gain a deeper level of understanding how it began in the first instance.

Patterns will become part of our conscious and subconscious mind and by us looking at the patterns in our life we can become aware of any areas in our life which seemed blocked.

Are we repeating the same cycle whilst fully aware that we don't seem to be moving forward?

By looking in depth at the patterns within our life we will be automatically placing ourselves in a position to change those which we feel either no longer serve us or never did.

The absolute truth is that if we do not begin to look at how we formed who we are now then we will never become the true person who chose to come to earth, we may well be a copy of somebody else's dreams or mistakes, we reserve the right to create our own patterns of behaviour and thoughtforms.

There is no room for ego in our earth journey to enlightenment and by removing parts of ourselves which may never have truly been ours in the beginning we can then become a clear channel, and only then, can we become a high functioning empath with the ability to gain power over our own lives and bring our true purpose work into fruition.

It is only during the journey of eradicating human patterns that we begin to work on our karmic imprint and many people are not aware enough of how tied these two situations are.

For those of you who do not understand the difference between the two a karmic pattern is created here on earth in this lifetime, and it is formed from our thoughts, emotions and repeated actions taken, if these patterns continue throughout the entire lifetime, they will play a part in creating a karmic imprint.

The creation of many lifetime's mistakes made and the forming of this within our Akashic records in turn creates a karmic imprint which will bring a new lesson and a new obstacle for us to overcome in any future lives therefore this will see us bring baggage back to earth upon our birth inevitably creating problems in this future lifetime for us to navigate.

For each lifetime that we fail to break down negative human patterns we are adding negative and low vibrational energy into our energy field which in turn overloads our system with a lower vibration, this will result in us having more to overcome to reach our higher vibrational level and this will undoubtedly not only repeat the patterns but transmute the pattern into karmic blocks.

By breaking down patterns you will be automatically working on your karmic imprint, many of my students and I have found that on our journey it is the Deep karmic work which has shown the most amazing and life changing results.

As empath's we must delve deep in order to truly find ourselves and whilst this is a tough journey which is capable of creating some difficult times for many people the journey to fully reconnect with our soul will bring life changing results.

I would always recommend a journal as it can be such a deep spiritual experience and journaling will assist you in navigating your way on this journey to the next level.

By focusing on one pattern at a time you will find that it begins to unravel more and without even looking further it will start to show a complex connection of patterns leading you to some amazing results, this is how we learn to find ourselves and understand ourselves at a deeper level.

You will gain an understanding of self-knowledge which up to now may well have been hiding from you. As you are unravelling the patterns which form your very existence remember to be kind to yourself, this is a spiritual process which can cause a lot of emotional upsets for you.

In order to gain self-growth, it is important that you really take your time in the process to understand your emotions along the way and to honour everything which becomes highlighted, understand the scars which you have gained along the way and the lessons which they have been part of. Always remember that we gain growth and learn from the difficult situations and try to remain grateful for them.

There may be times that you feel overwhelmed and at this point it will be important for you to just sit with the energy and gain understanding of it, this in turn helps to really understand what parts of you no longer serve you.

It is not important whether it takes six months or five years to fully eradicate any patterns which you feel do not belong to you because along the journey you will gain more growth in other areas.

If you feel you need to take a break for a while, then that is perfectly fine and this is a process which could take you many years to completely learn and understand about yourself so please do not try to rush to the finish line as if you do you won't truly be at the finish line.

The removal of ingrained patterns will illuminate who you truly are and along the way it will become more apparent to you of your reason for coming to earth.

We all came with a purpose and by allowing yourself to becoming the person you came to be your life purpose will unfold.

Mandy Wheeler

Chapter Six

RECONNECT TO YOUR SOUL

Each and every one of us made the decision to come to earth with a soul plan.

It is during our in-between lives state that we set in place the interactions and situations which will bring about real change and growth in our lives.

The in between lives state is a point in time after we have died from a previous life and before we are born into the next one and it is at this stage that our soul is capable of the clarity which is needed regarding what it requires in order to work on our karmic imprints, it is quite simple really and by understanding karma and past lives the reason for our time here on earth becomes a lot more crystal clear.

It is spiritual belief, and I am also shown from spirits who i have connected to in my work as a medium that after our death we return to source allowing for us to receive what is called a Life review.

Each and every one of us will be made aware of the impacts which we have had on the lives of Others and we will review any areas which we have not fulfilled our soul contracts which in turn may have created negative karma or at the very least stopped us from fulfilling the work we needed to do on any previous negative karma which we came with initially.

When we have failed to fulfil all of our soul contract obligations, we will automatically be placing karmic blocks within our energy field, and this will be creating an inconsistency within our vibrational field.

This is something which cannot undo itself without our soul input so at this life review we will begin preparing work on any new contracts which will assist us when we return to Earth. We must have connections with others, and this is where our soul family become relevant to us.

This is a group of souls who share similar energy and ties with each other and are known as our soul group, each one of us in this group will have already made the plan to interact with and influence each other's human lives at certain points which highlights the fact that everything is planned.

These souls are not all coming in with light and positive changes, some will bring trauma, distress, hurt and pain to facilitate our growth, these are our biggest lessons.

We will also experience our soulmate interaction which is destined to come at the point of awakening or to trigger awakening, many people expect this to be hearts and flowers however this is generally not the case.

Your soul mate will be somebody who pushes you past your limits and only if you do not connect to each other energetically in the desired way will this be a missed encounter resulting in an unalignment.

Alignment is paramount to keep the contract remaining

completely on track so they will be brought into your life again for the connection to be formed therefore it's very important for us to be aware of the people who are consistently placed in our life. For us to trigger reconnection we need to become spiritually aware and by doing so we have aligned ourselves with our plans even if our own mind is not yet aware of what these plans are.

By opening to our guides and becoming aware that this is a spiritual journey we will automatically be reconnecting to our soul, these are the points in our life when we will be raising our vibration as our energy begins to align with our plan, a plan which we came to earth with which will automatically connect us to those from our soul group.

This is not to say that we will be connecting to everybody from our soul family at this point all at the same time, as this was never part of the plan.

Before birth we set times and dates and we set situations for us to be placed in so that we will encounter each other at an exact point in time and be part of the story of each other's growth, in order for us to be part of that Trigger we must interact as we were always supposed to.

Nobody is accidentally placed in our life, and they may even seem to be bringing in life-changing destruction which takes us completely out of our comfort zone but all what we need to remember is to trust in the process and recognize that even the most destructive people in our life are part of our path.

They are part of our soul group and if we try to avoid being pulled in to the victim mentality which in turn will see us giving away our power we will learn to understand that we actually asked for all of this and our answers will become transparent, this will help us to navigate any problems much easier by being aware that this is only a lesson in part of our journey.

What makes this whole experience even more amazing is that we are born with our own guides along with a connection to our loved ones who have already passed over and even those of us who have not lost anybody close will still have descendants assisting us from the spirit world, all of these spirits help us along our path and help to highlight when we are supposed to be making changes and when we should be taking notice.

It is up to us to be aware enough and cleansed enough to take notice because a busy mind and a stressful life will lead you away from your spiritual path.

As we allow for ourselves to open up more and more spiritually our Guides and loved ones will be giving signs and whilst at first It may not be as obvious as we would like it to be it is up to us to become more spiritually aware and more adaptable as this will help to build a strength of relationship between us.

Repeated situations name or places will constantly be placed upon us in order for us to look deeper initially and as we begin to understand this more a relationship will build deeper with us and our guides. I will discuss how to connect to your guides in chapter nine and how to build a relationship with them.

The biggest thing which we must do in order to follow our spiritual path and reconnect to our soul will be to trust in ourselves and to trust in our guides I can assure you this is a skill which takes some fine tuning.

The main reason that most humans have become

disconnected from their soul and their guides is their inability to trust their inner guidance.

By allowing ourselves to train our brain to take a back seat our consciousness will be completely accessible to us allowing us a much easier and direct connection to our own soul.

It is our internal conditioning which we need to spend time on and once we do so we will become aware of the different types of patterns and blocks formed from the early years conditioning we have experienced.

We will therefore automatically raise our vibration with ease. I find that regular meditations and regular connection to our guides assists us to become more aligned with our soul.

HAVE YOU EVER QUESTIONED THE POSSIBILITY THAT YOU MAY HAVE GIVEN AWAY YOUR POWER?

Have you ever questioned the possibility that you may have given away your power?

This is one of the most important questions for an empath and the reason for this is because we do constantly give away our own power.

One of the biggest ways we give away our own energy and our own power is by us believing in the negative side of being an empath, the popular opinion is that we have no control over our energy and that anybody can drain our energy and there is absolutely nothing we can do about it.

By us adopting this way of thought we have automatically given away our power and we have now victimised ourselves.

In this mindset we have decided that we are no longer in charge of how our life is progressing and everybody who we interact with has a clear pathway to cause us destruction in some way and whilst I can understand how this mentality can be created because it is so difficult to live as an empath at times it is far from the truth.

As empaths we hold our own power and if we have subconsciously given this power away it is because we have done so through choice.

How many of us believe that we have to help whoever asks?

How many of us believe that we must put somebody else before ourselves?

Throughout points in our life every single one of us will answer yes to these questions, even an aware empath was once unaware, many of us believe that even though it is going to do us damage we are here on earth because we are supposed to help everybody.

This is the unhealed empath mentality and the reason for this is because we have been conditioned.

Although many of us were not aware of our empath ability as children and possibly throughout a large proportion of our adult life it does not negate the fact that we do have this ability, it does not change the fact that we always had this natural calling to help and to heal therefore the lack of knowledge and self-respect in this area coupled with the lack of lessons gained is what leads the empath to believe they are the victim within their own story.

We are obliged to look after our own energy above all else as our abilities are not only our empath power, but they are also our kryptonite and if we are to continuously ignore our own energy then we are undoubtedly leading ourselves onto a path of self-destruction.

If you feel that you have given away your power, then self-reflection is the most useful tool for you.

An empath's emotional survival depends on alone time as well as self-reflection, if we are not in a position to have space to self-reflect these situations it will cause suffering for us mentally, emotionally, physically and spiritually, the reason for this is that we are constantly channelling energy through our body so it is obvious that without the means to cleanse and heal the body regularly we will suffer.

Absorbing energy without cleansing will eventually cause us to be so heavily overloaded with the energy of others it will have a detrimental effect on our own healing,

it is important for an empath to keep their energy from becoming stagnant as when our energy becomes heavy with a lower vibrational energy it will cause our auric field to become sluggish and in turn this will lead to our aura slowing down and it will eventually stop spinning.

In its healthiest form our aura vibrates fast which creates a spinning effect and it is whilst our aura is spinning that it is protective to us and keeps it flowing with a higher vibration so nothing dense and heavy can stick to it whilst it is moving fast.

When we collect debris and negative experiences within our auric field this will cause a denser heavier vibration which will begin to slow it down and it is at this point that we are no longer living in our own vibration because we are now serving as the sponge that soaks up all of the energy which is attaching to us, here is the point that we become susceptible to attract more dense energy and negative experiences.

If you imagine a round ball moving fast nothing is really going to stick to it because it's going too fast but if you place that ball down and it is no longer moving it is now a stationary object which can be moved or damaged easily and this is exactly how the aura works,when it remains stationary it becomes vulnerable as it is not designed to be still and eventually over time this will manifest physical illnesses.

In order to retain our power it is important to maintain our own health,as empath's we spend too much time absorbing energy and stress through our body and without ensuring a constant flow of healthy energy we will always be at the mercy of outside energy.

Here are a few tips in order to keep your aura healthy.

- **a very long bath or swim twice a week- water is cleansing to an empath.**
- **daily grounding and protection.**
- **stay hydrated.**
- **meditate regularly.**
- **eat healthily- heavier food creates a denser energy field.**
- **exercise.**
- **energy healing.**
- **plenty of alone time.**
- **have a seat or a space which belongs to only you and nobody else comes into the space.**
- **spiritual practices and communication with your guides.**
- **getting enough sleep.**

By incorporating these into your routine you will begin to notice that your energy is gaining strength and this in turn will allow for you to when there is a more lower vibrational energy around you.

By working on yourself as discussed in previous chapters

alongside these self-care tips not only will you become more in touch with your own energy, but you will also learn to identify your own importance as well as identifying the importance of how other experiences are part of their karma.

Your support in their journey should be exactly that as opposed to taking their problems from them and making them your own which we all know is a common empath trait.

Self-study regarding who you give your power and your energy away to will eventually become as natural as breathing to you, but the early days will take a conscious effort of learning to pick everything apart as this is the only way for an empath to truly learn and hone their skills.

For you to start becoming aware of who you have given your energy to you must first be aware of the energy of all the people within your life so depending on how large your group is this could take anywhere between a couple of months to years as you will be going through a process with each person individually.

You will come to realize that the more time and attention you pay to somebody the more you will find yourself absorbing their energy which can take away your power or if we flip it you will actually be giving your power to that person, this is not necessarily because they are trying to take your power but because as an empath you are always subconsciously trying to solve everybody else's problems for them.

We are completely responsible for our part to play in this because it is us who is allowing it and only when we learn to understand our individual connections can we truly see our own responsibility in our actions therefore finally setting us free.

The first and most important step in taking back your own power is to learn to put your boundaries in place, when we establish boundaries, we are giving ourselves power over what we are willing to accept from people in our personal life as well as others who we interact with in all walks of life.

By setting these rules with ourselves we learn to stop our energy from being drained and we become more discerning of the battles we choose to face on behalf of others.

At some point every empath will feel like a victim to their own ability and this is to be expected but try not to live there, for those of you who wish to embrace this and use it as a stepping stone to your own power it is absolutely worth the journey and one day you will look back and question when you started putting yourself first because the process can sometimes be invisible.

Chapter Eight

PSYCHIC ATTACK

A psychic attack is when somebody is projecting negative emotions toward you whether it is intentional or not.

Sometimes we come into contact with people who either dislike us, hold some type of jealousy or envy towards us or feel any other number of negative emotions about us and this will generally lead to them sending us what is known as a psychic attack.

This psychic attack will result in the person lowering our vibrational energy system with their energy as it is not only their negative feelings which they project towards us but also their own general vibrational energy.

An empath will be more aware of this as they may notice the changes in their own energy, they will be more sensitive to feeling the thoughts and intentions of another towards them.

As the sender is harbouring these negative emotions it is fair to assume that their own vibrational energy will possibly be lower than yours, especially if you have been working on yourself and therefore this will automatically create inconsistencies within your own energy field and knock it out of alignment.

So we are in fact dealing with two separate issues here.

Firstly, we are dealing with the psychic attack. Secondly, we are dealing with the vibrational energy.

Understanding where the attack has come from is your priority, it will completely depend upon the strength of the person's negativity which will decipher the strength of the attack.

When we receive psychic attack, it will place blocks in front of us and this block will be formed from the low vibrational energy of the sender and will now alter your natural flow of energy resulting in blockages within your own experience.

This will cause your energy to become sluggish and in turn will bring in negative experiences, this will cause all lower vibrational energy to begin a run of bad luck which of course this will now in turn attract more of the same as this is how energy works, we will always attract what we create and as i have discussed previously a pattern can form if it goes unnoticed which will inevitably become a pattern of negative experiences because this energy which you are now projecting informs the universe that this is your new vibration.

The more visual empaths may well become aware of an energetic energy in their shoulder blades or in their back and this is usually a signal that the attacker is somebody who you would not expect to send it.

Psychic attack can cause physical signs in more sensitive empath's, and I find it can cause symptoms of feeling very drained and tired with a shaky feeling.

I have found that it usually takes three days for the full force of an attack to take hold for example if somebody begins to start thinking negatively toward you and projecting hatred or another negative emotion on a Sunday by Tuesday or Wednesday you will become aware of the results as your vibration will be low.

For those of you who are aware of your own energy the change will be more apparent than it will to those who are not.

In order to combat psychic attack, you must ensure that you were staying on top of your own psychic protection and shielding and whilst this will not stop an attack it will minimise the effects.

Keep your energy high which in turn will help to keep your vibration high, in order to do this it is important to eat lighter more healthy food and to avoid heavy starchy foods, swimming or exercising will help you to keep your vibration higher and meditation will also assist you.

clear quartz crystals will always lift your vibration as they are high vibration crystals and one of the best ways is to book yourself in for an energy healing which will become your best friend against psychic attack.

As a reiki and crystal therapy healer I am fully aware of the importance of energy healing.

Try to keep your thoughts loving and positive to the sender as opposed to returning a similar energy as this will only create a constant never-ending circle of negativity.

An empath's strongest point is to empathize and whilst it may seem difficult to empathize with somebody who is purposely hating on you it is important to remember that this person must be experiencing sadness or difficulties in their own life if they have such a low vibration.

Many people will disguise their fear and their weaknesses from themselves by projecting all of the negative and defensive emotions which they aim at you.

Maintaining a level of understanding as to why the attacker is the way they are will ultimately lead to forgiveness and forgiveness will lead to freedom.

It is important to remember that it is not only other people who send these attacks and it is important for us to be aware of the attacks that we ourselves can also accidentally send to our loved ones so try to catch yourself when you are feeling negative towards someone and work to turn the emotions into positive emotions.

When I notice that I am letting a negative feeling linger past the point that I have verbalized my discontent I will actively change the energy and on these occasions I will consciously remind myself to be mindful not to send out negative energy as feeling annoyed with somebody or angry with a loved one can become a bigger situation if you allow yourself to keep it going.

I often find by doing this that it clears the negative connection and allows me to think of all the positive things which I feel about this person.

The second issue at hand as mentioned earlier is that the sender has now placed their vibrational energy into your field which you can easily clear by having an energy healing.

You can get a good idea of who somebody is by sitting in this and observing their energy, not only is this a good exercise in learning to read energy but it also assists in becoming aware of how this specific person's energy affects you for future knowledge.

The most important thing to remember is that you are

always still in control and this is only a lesson in energy which will serve you well and it is also important to be aware that when somebody sends a psychic attack the person's own energy will always return back to them leaving them to deal with their own negative emotions.

Mandy Wheeler

Chapter Nine

ETHERIC CORDS AND HOOKS

An etheric cord is an invisible energetic cord of attachment from ourselves to another person or from ourselves to a situation.

An etheric cord can be positive or negative depending upon the situation and it allows a for a constant flow of energy back and forth between yourself and the other person.

When these cords are flowing positively, they will bring positive and loving relationships between you both.

You will find positive etheric cords within a happy relationship and also between parent and child, you will also find that they exist within healthy friendships and positive relationships with work colleague's.

However, on the other hand a negative etheric cord can be found within a toxic, negative or difficult relationship and the build-up of the negativity through the cords will eventually lead to a breakdown in the relationship.

Any relationships which have broken down will have

these negative cords within them and you will find that when somebody is finding it difficult to move on from a relationship which has ended they will automatically be attaching a negative etheric cord to you and without you having an awareness they will be in a position of power over you and you will be held back for moving forward into a new relationship.

For those of you have had a breakdown of a relationship or a divorce and you feel unable to detach yourself from this person regardless of whether you want to or not you would benefit from cutting and cleansing your etheric cords.

For somebody to create an etheric cord it is a simple as thinking about somebody regularly or creating an attachment to a person and this will create an energy link between you both.

For an empath this can become quite confusing and the reason for this is because we feel so deeply and can tend to feel the thoughts and emotions of others very strongly through these cords.

It is quite possible for these cords to be manipulated and for anybody who does understand etheric cords then this can become quite apparent to the empath as their level of reading the energy being sent to them will alert them to a definite problem being created.

If you are having difficulties in any of your key relationships which you would like to improve then working on your cords and hooks will be the perfect place for you to start.

When we experience negative emotions or situations with those whom we love and care for we are in fact sending a lower vibrational energy through the cords to each other which results in the disharmony between you growing bigger.

By being aware that you are in fact contributing to the downfall of this particular relationship you can begin the process of repairing the damage which you are creating, you can do this by cleansing this particular cord as opposed to removing it.

For us to cleanse the cord we use colours which contribute to the breaking down of low vibrational energy therefore allowing for us to restore this negative energy to its previous positive and loving state.

To begin this process find yourself a relaxed space where you will not be disturbed, put on some soft relaxation music and i find it helpful to spend a few minutes practising my breathing techniques, when you feel ready ask for your guides to please begin loving healing on your cords between yourself and the specific person whom you wish to repair the relationship with.

First ask for them to send love down this cord accompanied by a vibrant pink light, imagine that you are watching this pink light flow gently up and down the cord and as you do so picture the person in your mind glowing in this same pink light, whilst you are creating this loving space between you both let yourself remember all of the loving and happy moments that you have shared as this will fill the cord with all of the positive and caring energy which lies beneath the arguments and the upset.

When you are confident that you have completed this step then you are ready to move to the next stage which is to follow the exact same process but with a gold light.

The gold light will provide a strength back into the cord

whilst forcing the spiritual connection between you both, it is important to repeat the process at regular intervals to ensure a healthy relationship is maintained.

Becoming aware of negative cords and hooks which we ourselves have attached to somebody is vital in order for us to be proactive in our healthy cord work.

We must accept responsibility when we ourselves are relying too heavily on somebody else as this can result in us putting up a hook which I mainly see on those who tend to be quite responsible for somebody else's experience.

In circumstances where somebody is either forced to or actively chooses to become heavily reliant on us it will inadvertently attach a cord to us that includes a hook and the purpose for this is that they are under the misconception that they need us as they are choosing to give away their own power.

We can maintain the health of our own cords which we have connected to others by regaining our own power and always being very aware and very honest with ourselves, in regards to relying on other people if you are self-aware and able to identify a relationship in your life where this is happening it will be important that you introduce boundaries into this particular relationship.

By introducing boundaries, you are energetically preparing the person of the changes which you wish to make beforehand so that when you actively remove the cord and hook, they will not instantly feel the need to reattach it this will allow for a healthy flow of energy between you both.

When you remove the negative energy and the hook from the cord if this is a relationship which should remain it can now flow with positive loving and balanced energy back and forth.

Being overly reliant on somebody completely strips away your Power by automatically allowing that other person to hold power over you, there are times we that believe people need us to function and the more that we enable this behaviour the weaker that person will actually become and it is us that is key in facilitating this.

When we become enablers, we are in fact taking responsibility for the energy of somebody else which in turn will cause us to build resentment and create a negative and a lower vibrational energy which automatically causes damage to the cords.

When we break down relationships in this way it becomes clearly apparent to us that we are making the choice to give away our own energy and to take the energy of others into our own experience.

By practicing mindfulness and boundaries, we can make a real change to this and can ensure that we are not only allowing ourselves to be fully in charge of our own power but we are also assisting others to do the same.

In order to cleanse negative etheric cords it is important to allow for yourself to be aware and honest of any negative relationships or situations which you are involved in, the truth is that we subconsciously allow for most of our negative attachments and we convince ourselves that we are powerless in these as we get into the" I don't have a choice" mindset.

We always have a choice, and we do not have to be constantly drained or responsible for the energy of others even if our human conditioning tells us otherwise.

To begin this process you must first identify the cord and

once you have done so please allow for yourself to mentally make peace with this person or with this situation, you must also be prepared and ready to let go as is only when we are willing to let go of whatever does not serve us and put the outcome in the hands of our guides or the universe that we can remove all which should no longer be.

To repeat the same process of relaxation, find a quiet space where you will not be disturbed and put on some quiet and relaxing music, now ask for your guides to come forward and to cut all negative etheric cords.

At this stage allow for yourself to release all control of what you would like to happen and let yourself accept that they will remove cords which will assist in your growth, if you are quite visual picture the cords and allow for yourself to see them in whichever visual form they show and then release them to the universe.

It is beneficial to repeat this cord cutting process as regularly as once a week and then just sit back and allow for your life to become exactly what it was supposed to be.

Mandy Wheeler

Chapter Ten

KARMIC CLEANSING

What is karma?

Our karma is the energy which we create returning to meet us. What this means is that the energy which we give out and the actions which we take are created by us and we must always receive back identical energy to that which we project out into the world and live by.

Many people seem to be under the impression that karma is something which happens to us, but this is not the correct interpretation of karma.

The karma which we create is directly returned to us in the same form of the energy which we are giving out, so for example if we are being cruel and nasty to people, we will be receiving the same type of person into our experience as what we give out, we must receive back.

It is guaranteed that if we are attracting people with a negative and toxic mindset into our experience that we will be attracting negative experiences.

When we intentionally cause or wish negative experiences or harm on others, we are in fact bringing this into our own lives as we will always receive back the same vibrational energy which we are resonating at.

Negative emotions and actions are low vibrational energy so therefore if we ourselves are experiencing them then we are living in a low vibrational energy and must receive back the same frequency.

When we are resonating at a high frequency it stands to reason that we will receive back the same high vibrational energy which will be positive experiences and situations.

So, you see the creation of our karma is completely in our own hands and by us living in a positive state of mind we must receive back the same positive experiences.

When we become aware that we do in fact create our own energy then life becomes a lot simpler for us and it is our responsibility to become the mindful creator in our own experience as we are now no longer ignorant to the fact that we are in charge.

When we begin to fully understand how we create karma we can therefore allow for ourselves to navigate any negative karma which we have accumulated quite easily and by becoming grateful to it for mirroring where we are on our journey back to us it can help to process your past karma faster.

By processing past karma almost instantly it brings us knowledge of self and this in turn assists on our journey of growth, we cannot escape karma, but we can use it as the tool it is intended to be and observe our own patterns and behaviours through it if we are honest with ourselves about our shadows and our true self.

When we begin to become an active participant in cleaning up old and creating new karma, we become more aware of what we are creating, and this allows for us to understand energy and for us to learn the lesson at a soul level.

To cleanse our karma acknowledgement is key, how can we possibly change ourselves for the better if we are not willing to identify the negative aspects of ourselves and our actions, each and every one of us will have created some negative karma for ourselves at some point in our life.

Take each karmic situation at a time and allow for yourself to truly understand the lesson which is being brought to you and in doing this it will lead to the raising of your vibration and a cleansing of that karmic pattern.

By removing negative karma, we leave a space for us to create positive karma in its place so try not to only focus on what you are removing, it is important to also focus on the positive growth which this particular lesson is teaching you.

In order to heal your karma, you must be aware of any repeated patterns in your life which constantly recur, and it is only when we move past our victim mentality that we can truly understand what lies beneath these patterns.

By uncovering a karmic pattern, it enables self-knowledge of our shadows which we may have uncovered whilst working through this book.

On many occasions past life regression will be helpful in the removal of negative karma as it can be created over more than one lifetime and if you were not spiritually aware in a previous life you would have allowed negative karmic patterns to be added to your karmic imprint.

In my work as a regression therapist, it is impossible to ignore the similarities between my client's previous lives and their present life, they seem to highlight similar journeys and obstacles to overcome which reinforces the pattern of repeated karma becoming an imprint which we carry throughout subsequent lives.

I have had clients who have chosen regression to be their regular main healing tool to change their present life and it is an amazing transformation of their life as we literally work through their hurdles and blocks in this way.

When we have removed the negative karma which we have created for ourselves in this lifetime we will then be directed to work on our imprint, and this is when regression is extremely powerful in this final stage of healing.

We change our karma by changing our energy and whilst we must work through any karma which we have created prior to becoming energy conscious we should become aware that what we are creating from this moment onwards will allow for us to become an active participant in the new karma which we are consciously creating moving forward.

We must not forget that we are consistently always creating karma and the most important thing to remain mindful of is that we are responsible for the karma which we have created and the only way for us to remove any negative karma is by receiving it with grace.

Mandy Wheeler

_____
_____
_____
_____
_____
_____
_____
_____
_____
_____
_____
_____
_____
_____
_____
_____
_____
_____
_____
_____
_____
_____
_____
_____
_____
_____
_____
_____
_____

Chapter Eleven

CONNECTING TO YOUR GUIDES.

Our guides are the key to us navigating life on earth in the way that was intended when we made the decision to come here, they are here to guide and assist us in our journey on earth.

When our soul made the decision to come to earth there was a whole network of soul's involved in the planning of this and our guides were the biggest part of this network, they are here to accompany us and to guide us on our journey and this is their soul's purpose.

Guides are personal to us and have no interest in any other human's journey as they are specifically our own guides unlike angels and other beings who assist in the greater good for humanity in general.

I have the utmost respect and gratitude to my guides, and I would like to think that they are aware of this as without them I would not have navigated my journey in the way which I have, and I most definitely would not have gained the knowledge or level of understanding which I now have.

As a psychic and as a healer I am completely aware that it is my guides who do all the legwork, and my only job is to keep my body and mind cleansed enough to directly receive the messages.

To function spiritually as an empath our guides input is critical, they create our protection and from the moment which we allow for them to guide us on our journey they will be instrumental in creating our path.

This chapter will cover how to create the connection and build the relationship with your guides so that you can work together in creating the life of your dreams.

Your first step is to get yourself into a quiet space where you will not be disturbed, then just allow for yourself to have a clear mind, this stops any confusion for your guides.

Your guides are unable to actively participate in your life until you make them aware that you wish for them to do so, this is due to free will, in order to let them know that you now wish for them to begin guiding you it is as simple as telling them, you can either do this in your mind through thought or you can ask them out loud to" please begin guiding you now in life".

Once you have made them aware of this you need to find an easy way of communication for you whilst you are building this relationship.

To facilitate communication at this stage i would always suggest a pendulum which will become a little bit like a telephone between you or the second option is automatic writing.

Automatic writing is my main form of communication

alongside talking to them however when we built our relationship up in the early days i used a pendulum and this has assisted the growth and led to a direct communication of words and conversations now.

You will need to order yourself a pendulum if you do not have one however you can use anything which you find to hand to serve as a pendulum if you do not have one and wish to begin straight away, for example a necklace or a bracelet.

Firstly, hold the pendulum in your dominant hand (the hand which you write with) between thumb and forefinger and ask your guides either in your mind or out loud to please show you your yes - you will receive a response by the pendulum swinging a specific way and this will always be your yes.

Repeat the same question and ask to be shown a no and again you will receive a response from your pendulum swinging a different way, this will always be your no.

Finally repeat the same question but this time asking for your guides to show you a maybe/ don't know, this answer will be something which you will only receive when your guides can not provide a definite yes or no.

These responses will always be the same from your guides as they will be consistent in their answers and the reason that it is important to firstly set your answers is to ensure that it is your guides who you are contacting.

There are lower vibrational entities and spirits which will also become quite interested in any communication which they may intercept and by you becoming aware of your guides answer's it will lead you to practice communication safely, if your answers are different from what you have set with your guides and inconsistent then do not communicate and perhaps move to another room or leave it for the time being.

Once you have set these answers it is now time to start creating a bond with your guides, I always recommend running some of your plans for the day or ideas that you have past your guides and the reason for this is that you are building communication, it doesn't matter whether you can hear them at this point, what matters is that they are learning how to communicate with you.

They will attempt different ways of responding and this will be a learning curve for them on how perceptive you are, it will ultimately lead to both sides gaining stronger levels of understanding.

Automatic writing is a lot easier than it may seem at first and it is my absolute favourite, i find that my guides can predict and answer questions for me with so much clarity, however it does take a bit of practice in order to fully shut off your mind and allow for your hand to automatically channel that which it is being led to write.

I will always get myself in to a space where I don't need to think about anything else at that time and just allow for myself to write, I suggest that you practice this and keep it all in a journal which you can come back to at later dates, this will allow for you to become aware of situations which do happen and it helps to clarify your guides way of predicting.

As you progress through your spiritual journey your guides will be constantly placing new situations in your path, they were planned before you came here and was always going to be part of the journey.

By giving up control you will be placing yourself in the

exact position which you are supposed to be in because your guides remember why you came as well as all of the situations which are supposed to lead you to your soul purpose, it is much more difficult than it sounds to completely give up control over our own life in order to be led by someone that you cannot see but I assure you that it is definitely worth it and will lead to great places if you can manage to place this level of trust in them.

You have more than one guide, you have a teacher guide, a guardian angel and a life guide, you also have a gatekeeper and depending on whether you work spiritually there will also be healing guides and separate psychic guides who will enter your life.

Learning to connect to each guide individually over time will help you to differentiate who is trying to bring you answers and what they are trying to guide you towards at that stage and this in turn will create a way for you to move forward with ease.

An important process to follow when you are working spiritually in any way is to ensure that you are grounded and that you are practising psychic protection, which I find can be done simply by using the pendulum.

Ask your guides to ground you and keep your mind focused whilst doing so, this will be answered by the pendulum showing your yes, allow for your pendulum to swing until they have completed the task and then repeat the process by asking for protection in a bubble of gold or white light all around the body, please ensure this bubble is encasing the whole body including beneath the feet.

Another good way to protect yourself is to imagine a bright gold or white shield in front of you and as you walk closer to it in your mind's eye watch how the shield grows and morphs to fit your body shape as it fully encases your body, become aware that it shines a bright light outwards warding off all negative energy.

Finally please ensure that you are always looking for new ways in which your guides will be communicating with you and the reason for this is that as your relationship strengthens and grows so will your vibration and this will lead to your ability to communicate becoming a lot clearer.

Chapter Twelve

THE EMPATH PARTNER

For those people who have an empath in their life, sometimes it can seem very difficult for several reasons.

If your relationship is going to survive it is important for you to become fully aware of how an empath works.

Your empath partner is full of love and care for humanity and needs to be able to express this, some partners are threatened by this and need to feel that their empath is consumed with love for them alone, this relationship will never work as you cannot hold an empath down and by doing so they will become a stunted and toxic version of themself.

An empath must be in a relationship with somebody who is completely comfortable with themselves and does not need validation.

Your empath partner will be tuned in to your thoughts and emotions and this can lead to a very intense and deep relationship, your empath will know any subtle changes that is within your vibrational field and your thoughts so this can only ever be a relationship based on complete honesty for it to flourish and continue.

Because an empath is so in tune with you they will intuitively understand what could make any situations you are in easier for you and this can be frustrating as it may seem that they are controlling, an empath has to work hard to try to remember that they cannot solve everybody's problems and this is something they must learn in order to not take the power away from their partner.

An aware empath understands the importance of respecting their partner's right to privacy and independence, they will offer a support system with their gifts as opposed to invading their partner's life with control.

When an empath partner understands themselves and has completed the work necessary on their own inner problems, they will understand the importance of their partner's growth and how they must support them in attaining it whilst stepping back from trying to do it for them.

It can become very difficult and frustrating to understand what an empath is enduring daily and sometimes it may feel easier to try to close off and not acknowledge what they are going through.

With the channelling of energy, the world can feel like a lonely place for them sometimes and you are their light in the storm. The stronger your relationship is the more of an anchor you will become for them which allows for them to feel truly safe in your energy.

It is when the empath feels that they are becoming a burden that you will become aware of how they will close off from you and this will lead to them self-isolating.

Communication is so very important to your empath as they built on emotions and sensitivity, their complete design is to help others so if they feel that for whatever reason they are being forced to shut down this will have a very negative impact on them.

When an empath is channelling somebody else's energy, it can sometimes continue over a period of days or even week's if the person whose energy they have absorbed is a consistent energy in them.

This can be for any number of reasons, and this can become confusing and disorientating for the empath so at these times you will need to be understanding and try not to take their change of emotions or behaviour personally, it is best to allow them to spend time alone to recharge as that will be the key to them cleansing their energy.

An empath will be the most loving and caring partner you could ever wish to have who will love you with their whole being and if you are willing to understand your empath and really listen to them you will find that you are in a relationship which is based on the purest love which you could ever know here on earth.

Mandy Wheeler

Mandy Wheeler

Printed in Great Britain
by Amazon